The Fruit of the Spirit

Judith Tamasang Jogwuia
Illustrated by Mukah Mukah Ispahani

The Fruit of the Spirit

Visit www.childrenwant2know.com

Copyright © 2021 by Judith Tamasang Jogwuia

All rights reserved. No part of this publication may be reproduced, distributed, or transmitted in any form or by any means, including photocopying, recording, or other electronic or mechanical methods, without the prior written permission of the author, except in the case of brief quotations embodied in critical reviews and certain other non-commercial uses permitted by copyright law.

Scripture quotations taken from the Holy Bible, New Living Translation, copyright 1996, 2004. Used by permission of Tyndale House Publishers, Inc., Wheaton, Illinois 60189. All rights reserved.

Scripture quotations are from The Holy Bible, English Standard Version® (ESV®), copyright © 2001 by Crossway, a publishing ministry of Good News Publishers. Used by permission. All rights reserved.

Tellwell Talent
www.tellwell.ca

ISBN
978-0-2288-5839-3 (Hardcover)
978-0-2288-5838-6 (Paperback)
978-0-2288-5970-3 (eBook)

Table of Contents

Acknowledgements v
Author's Note vii
Introduction ix
1   Three Persons in One God 1
2   The Person of the Holy Spirit 9
3   The Holy Spirit Produces Fruit in Me 17
4   The Holy Spirit and Me 21
5   The Fruit of the Spirit is … Love 29
6   The Fruit of the Spirit is … Joy, Peace 35
7   The Fruit of the Spirit is … Patience 41
8   The Fruit of the Spirit is … Kindness, Goodness 45
9   The Fruit of the Spirit is … Faithfulness 49
10 The Fruit of the Spirit is … Gentleness 53
11 The Fruit of the Spirit is … Self-Control 56
12 Afterword 61

Acknowledgements

To God, my Father, my All, who inspired this book, by the power of the Holy Spirit through Christ Jesus.

To Venbing, my calm and steady half. Thank you for your unwavering love and support.

To Alex, Ari, and Daniel, whom God used to bring this book to life.

To my Father-in-Faith and mentor, Prophet Austin Idahosa, whom God continues to use to grow my spiritual life.

To Prophet Samuel King Tataw, for humbly allowing God to use you call me.

To Recreation Fire and Miracles Ministries, which sows seeds of God's Word in His little children. May the Holy Spirit use you more to produce fruit in them, continuously.

Author's Note

Dear Reader,

We're so glad you're here!

As mentioned, this book will take you on an adventure to discover God the Holy Spirit as the invisible Friend and Helper, who can enable and teach you anything, as well as bear fruit in you.

It shares practical ways in which you can invite God into your daily activities to empower you to bear the fruit of good moral qualities like love, joy, peace, and much more, so that you can live a happy and satisfying life.

Special features include bible memory verses that aim to build a mental library of God's truths about you, and reflections that will reinforce your learning.

As you open your mind to understand, and as you stay grounded in God's truths about who He created you to become, you will be equipped with confidence in your identity in God and the resilience needed to handle the tough challenges that life will inevitably bring your way.

Most importantly, you will be launched into a new realm of unbelievable possibilities and be enabled to blossom into your newly found virtues and abilities.

All of this is possible when you dare to believe in God's truths and build a close relationship with the Holy Spirit, who is the power of God that works within you.

Rest assured that the Holy Spirit will be there to help you all the way. So, perhaps we should get to know Him a little better.

Now, will you join us on this adventure to explore further?

Introduction

Hello!

I'm Alex.

I learnt about the Fruit of the Spirit at Sunday School in church, and I'm eager to know more.

I learnt that the Holy Spirit has good fruit that can grow in me and make me become the good and extraordinary person that God created me to be. That's fascinating!

I have many questions about this, like... who is the Holy Spirit? And I thought fruits only grew on plants?

Grown-ups know a lot of things... I think I'll ask my parents.

I'm on an adventure to learn all that I can about the Fruit of the Spirit.

Will you join me?

Galatians 5:22–23
"BUT THE FRUIT OF THE SPIRIT IS:
LOVE, JOY, PEACE,
PATIENCE, KINDNESS, GOODNESS,
FAITHFULLNESS, GENTLENESS AND SELF CONTROL.
AGAINST SUCH THINGS THERE IS NO LAW."

1
THREE PERSONS IN ONE GOD

"First things first! To understand who the Holy Spirit really is," Dad said, "first, you must understand who God is."

Dad told me that God created the heavens and the earth. God also created me to look like Him. He created you too. So, we are all God's children. And God loves us very much.

We have biological parents on earth, but God is our spiritual parent.

"Because you are God's beloved child," Dad said to me, "you are a royal child. And God has given you the authority to rule over His kingdom here on earth on his behalf."

"That is really cool!" I replied.

"Imagine what great things you can achieve on earth, Alex, as a royal child of God, the King of heaven and earth, "he said.

I thought about it... I am the King's child! I am special. You're special too.

Kings rule kingdoms. My curious mind wondered where God's kingdom is, and what His crown looked like... perhaps gold, diamond, or silver?

Dad explained that God is the King of heaven and earth. He sits on His throne in heaven, and rules over both heaven and the earth.

"But God's kingdom is different from other kingdoms," Dad noted. "He rules with love, patience and justice. God wants His children to love everyone the same way He loves us."

I learnt that God is the one, true, living God. He is holy, meaning unique or different. And there is no other god like Him.

Dad said that God is a Spirit. And that there are three persons in One God: Father, Son and Holy Spirit. This is also called the Holy Trinity.

Tri-means three, so three persons working together, in unity, as one gigantic God.

"So God is a three-in-one God. He must be very powerful," I thought.

Dad further explained this mystery to me.

"God the Father is our spiritual Father in heaven. We are all God's children.

Jesus is the first-born Son of God, whom God sent from heaven to earth. He died for our sins to save us from facing eternal death in hell, after our lives here on earth.

And finally, God is present on earth and rules the world through the power of the Holy Spirit."

"So, the Holy Spirit is the presence and power of God on earth?" I asked.

"That's right! Think about it this way," he said. "God, the Father is like the sun. He shines His light from out of space, in heaven, and lights up the world every day, bringing daylight out of the earth's darkness.

Jesus is the Light of the world. We experience the Father's love on earth through the Light (Jesus) of the sun rays that we receive.

Just as plants need sunlight to grow, without which they will die, we all need Jesus, the Light of God, in our lives to grow and bear fruit."

"However, Alex," Dad continued, "you must open the curtains of your heart and let the light of Jesus come in, so that every darkness in your life can give way to the Light. If you want to experience joy and blessings here on earth, you must make room for Jesus in your heart".

"My heart?" I asked.

"How can Jesus live in my heart?"

"Your spiritual heart," he responded, smiling at my naiveite. "It is a virtual part of your body - like a cloud, that powers your thoughts, emotions and will. Often, our hearts are controlled by bad thoughts. But if you ask Jesus to forgive you and come rule your heart, then the Holy Spirit will come live in you and help you think and act like Jesus, your new Lord. He will teach you God's will – the right way God wants you to live.

Plus, if you keep living God's way, you will go to heaven and live happily ever after death. There's life after death on earth, you know."

"God the Father, Son and Holy Spirit are one," Dad said. "We can't see God because He is invisible. The Holy Spirit is how God lives in us."

This is fascinating! I want the light of Jesus in my heart so that I can live a good and happy life. Who wouldn't want to be happy?

"Jesus, please come into my heart now, and be Lord over my life," I cried.

How about you? Do you want to be happy, too? Do you want to go to heaven and live forever? Ask Jesus to come and rule your heart, now.

Later that night, in my bed, I mused over all the interesting things that Dad had told me earlier.

So, there are three persons in one God: Father, Son and Holy Spirit. And because I asked Jesus to come into my heart, the Holy Spirit now lives in me. He will help me know and become more like Jesus. He will help me live God's way so that I can live a good and happy life that pleases God. Oh, how I love Jesus!

"I want to know more about the Holy Spirit," I thought, as I dozed off.

Prayer: Dear God, my Father, thank you for creating me. Jesus, thank you for coming into my heart. Please shine your light in me and through me. Holy Spirit help me know God and the ways of God more. I ask this in the name of Jesus. Amen.

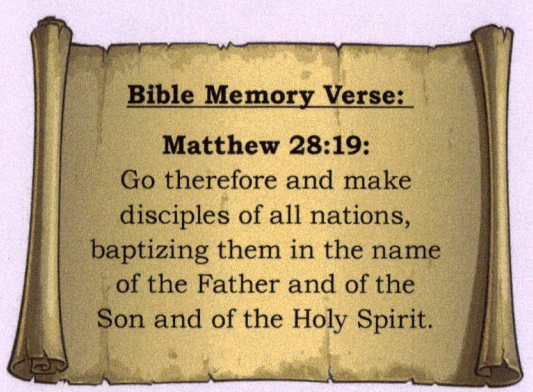

Bible Memory Verse:

Matthew 28:19:
Go therefore and make disciples of all nations, baptizing them in the name of the Father and of the Son and of the Holy Spirit.

REFLECTION:
Who is God? How many persons are there in one God?

2
THE PERSON OF THE HOLY SPIRIT

The next day, I was doing my daily morning chores as usual, sweeping the floor, tidying up my room, and all the not-so-fun stuff. You see, I'd rather be playing, but Mom said I should work before playing.

"Mom," I called, as I swept the kitchen floor, "can you please tell me more about the Holy Spirit? I learnt that He can help me know God more and make me become more like Jesus.

Who is He? How does He help?"

"Of course, Alex," she replied.

"God created us to have a father-and-child relationship with Him. The Holy Spirit helps connect us with God.

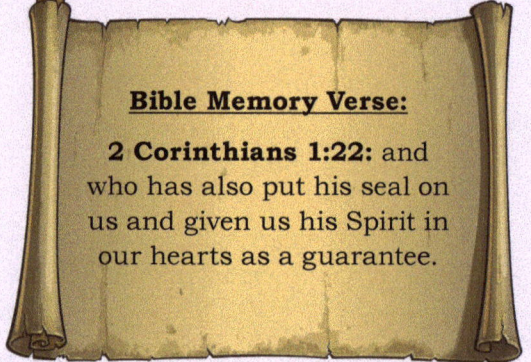

Bible Memory Verse:

2 Corinthians 1:22: and who has also put his seal on us and given us his Spirit in our hearts as a guarantee.

The Holy Spirit is the third person of the three-in-one God. Like God the Father and Jesus, God the Son, He too is Lord.

When the Holy Spirit lives in us, He connects God's children to Jesus, and the Father, who are one. That means that we become the walking presence of God on earth when we have the Holy Spirit in us."

"That's mind blowing!" I responded.

"You see," Mom continued, "the Holy Spirit is also the power of God in us. He gives us power to love the way God wants His children to love, power to help people and power to become who God created us to be.

God wants His children to love everyone and to do good to people so that the world can see His beautiful kingdom on earth through our lives and be drawn to Him.

Even if you find it hard to love and help others naturally, the Holy Spirit can change you. He enables you to think and act like Jesus."

"How does He do that?" I asked, curious to know even more.

"For example," Mom replied, you can't see electricity, but if you plug a computer cable into a socket, it powers up the computer and enables it to work the way it was built to function.

This is how the Holy Spirit empowers you. He makes you willing and able to do the things that God wants you to do – even the things you think you can't do.

You see, with God, nothing is impossible!

The Holy Spirit communicates the will of God, our Father in heaven, to His children on earth.

He usually speaks to you with a gentle voice. You can hear His voice, like the sound of your mind, when you pray or meditate on God's Word – the Bible.

He can even drop a good thought or idea in your heart. He helps you understand clearly what God wants."

"And when you obey Him, God is pleased and He blesses you," she added.

"I see. I want God to be happy with me. Is that why you asked me to read my bible, and to pray and meditate first thing every morning?" I asked.

"Correct! God speaks to us through the Bible too. The Holy Spirit helps you understand God's will for your life, and He leads you in God's way," she answered.

"Plus, early mornings are quieter, so you can focus more easily.

Have you been praying in the mornings, Alex?"

"Only sometimes, I'm afraid," I replied. "But I want the Holy Spirit to lead me in God's way. I'll do my best to be more consistent. From tomorrow, I'll try to wake up early every morning to pray and meditate."

"That's a great decision," Mom answered, smiling. "I can tell that the Holy Spirit just convicted you."

"The Holy Spirit convicted me?" I repeated slowly, trying to understand what Mom meant.

"Yes. That's another way He works, you know. He makes you willing, so that you want to do the right thing. Then He enables you to do it. He's awesome like that!

I pray that He gives you the power to turn your words into action."

"Sometimes, the Holy Spirit can speak directly into your ears. Like a person, you can have a conversation with Him if you make Him your friend.

He can also give you a message or an instruction through a dream or a vision.

The Holy Spirit can even use people to talk to you - just like He inspired me to talk to you to do the right thing, just now. He can make your parents, preachers, teachers, or even a stranger, give you the right instruction that can keep you from trouble, or guide you to make the right decision in a tough situation, or even lead you to discover your purpose in life – what God created you to do on earth.

You see, Alex, God created everyone on earth for a special assignment. Typically, the good things that you do well with just a little effort would be in line with your purpose. The Holy Spirit can help you discover why you were born. He will guide you to make choices that align with your purpose. When you follow His leading, He will steer you towards the right path and you will live a happy life."

"But Mom, how can I tell if it is really the Holy Spirit talking to me through someone?" I asked, worried. "What if someone is lying to me?"

"Oh, you will know, my love," she replied. "The Holy Spirit is the Spirit of Truth. He'll make you know truth from lies. If you're not sure, you can pray, even in your mind, and ask Him to lead you in the way you should go.

When you obey His instructions, things work out well for you in the end. He makes even impossible things happen... when you obey.

There are other ways to confirm the voice of the Holy Spirit. Apart from making you want to do God's will, He'll enable you, and you'll feel happy when you do it. If you don't obey first time, He'll remind you – maybe through a thought, a dream or even someone.

He will also help you make good decisions. Even if you get in trouble, God will always help you, especially when you pray.

You see child, the Holy Spirit is your Helper and your Teacher of everything."

"I'm grateful to God for giving me the Holy Spirit," I responded.

"I do need help, Mom."

"Don't we all, my dear?" said Mom.

"Everybody needs help sometimes... everybody."

Prayer: Dear Holy Spirit, please help me discover my purpose on earth. Show me the will of God for my life and lead me in the right path. In the name of Jesus, I pray. Amen.

Bible Memory Verse:

John 14: 26: But the Helper, the Holy Spirit, whom the Father will send in my name, he will teach you all things and bring to your remembrance all that I have said to you.

REFLECTION:

How does the Holy Spirit communicate God's will to His children?

List three things that the Holy spirit can help you do.

3

THE HOLY SPIRIT PRODUCES FRUIT IN ME

I didn't realize when my morning chore time had turned into a teaching session. But I didn't mind because I was learning a lot of good lessons.

Mom also taught me that if I continue to allow the Holy Spirit to lead me, rather than do things my own way, He will produce fruit in my life.

"You mean, like real fruit that grows on plants?" I asked.

"This fruit is different," she smiled. "It shows in your life in the form of moral virtues or good behavior that represent the nature of God. Remember, we are all created in God's image.

The Bible talks about nine of them: love, joy, peace, patience, kindness, goodness, faithfulness, gentleness, and self-control.

You see, the Fruit of the Spirit is the evidence that God lives in you. This is important. Just as apple trees produce apples, God expects His children to behave like Him, just like Jesus did when He was on earth."

"I see," I said thoughtfully. "God created me in His image, so I must behave in a way that when people see me, they will see God's good nature."

"That's right!" Mom said. "God wants us to spread His love and to apply the Golden Rule as we relate with other people."

"What is the golden rule?" I asked.

"Treat everyone the way you want to be treated," she answered.

"One way to achieve this is to always ask yourself, when you need to make any decision: 'what would Jesus do?'

Jesus is the example we must always follow."

"You see, just as fruit is tasty and attractive," she added, "so too when you do good to people, and display the Fruit of the Spirit, you will make a positive impact in people's lives as they experience God's love through you. In this way, more people will be drawn to live God's way too.

Imagine a world where everyone treated everyone else with love. There would be no pain, no wars, no death - just as it is in heaven."

"Is that really how heaven is?" I asked eagerly.

"Yes, my dear. And this is how God wants His kingdom on earth to be.

God is counting on his disciples, Alex - followers like you and I - to bring His heavenly kingdom rule to the earth. Each of us must do our part to achieve this."

"But Mom, how? That sounds like a gigantic responsibility," I cried.

"Well, through the power of the Holy Spirit, who is at work within you. Don't forget that you have the Holy Spirit, who is your Helper and Teacher. He adds the 'super' to your natural abilities. He can make you do even what you think is impossible!

You just make sure you always obey the voice of the Holy Spirit and ask Him to help you whenever you need help. He always answers when we call Him.

When you listen to His voice and obey Him, He will lead you in the right path and the Fruit of the Spirit will grow in you. Okay, Alex?"

"Okay. Thanks, Mom. I learnt a lot today." I said.

"I love you, Mom."

"I love you too, my darling," Mom responded, and gave me a big hug.

Later that night in my bed, I was excited as I thought about all that I had learnt. I think I heard Mom say that the Holy Spirit could turn me into a super-human. Superman? I smiled at the thought of having superpowers.

That night I prayed:

"Dear Lord, I'm so glad that I learnt about your Holy Spirit. I want my life to show the Fruit of the Spirit. Holy Spirit fill me up, please.

Let the fruit of love, joy, peace, patience, kindness, goodness, faithfulness, gentleness, and self-control grow in me. In the name of Jesus, I pray. Amen."

Bible Memory Verse:

John 15: 5: I am the vine; you are the branches. Whoever abides in me and I in him, he it is that bears much fruit, for apart from me you can do nothing.

REFLECTION:

Read Galatians 5:22-23 every day this week and memorize the verses. What are the virtues of the Fruit of the Spirit?

4

THE HOLY SPIRIT AND ME

Normally, Mom would wake me up every day to prepare for school. But today, I woke up with a jolt - very early before she came.

I felt like someone woke me up. Could it be the Holy Spirit?

Before reading my favorite psalm from my Bible, Psalm 23, I prayed that the Holy Spirit would help me understand.

"He leads me in the path of righteousness, for His name's sake...," I paused and thought about it. Suddenly, my lips opened up, and I said: "Lord, I know you are here. Please lead me in the right path today."

Then I had a light bulb moment. I realized that the Holy Spirit had just led me to pray according to the Word of God, which is the will of God.

I was filled with energy. I felt good. I was ready to start my day!

Next, I decided to do my house chores early before school time.

Mom walked into the kitchen to make breakfast and saw me sweeping the floor.

"Look who's doing their chore without a reminder," she teased. "I'm proud of you, my love!"

I think I also heard her whisper the words: "Praise Jesus!" as she walked towards the fridge for some milk.

"Mom," I called, "you said the Holy Spirit connects us with God and leads us according to God's will, right?"

"Hmm hmm..." she replied.

"I think I experienced that this morning." I said. "While meditating on Psalm 23, I felt like someone was present, even though I couldn't see who. I even felt comfortable talking - like to a real friend."

"That's the Holy Spirit alright – the presence of God with you. I bet your Bible passage made sense to you too."

"Yes! How did you know?" I responded in surprise. "I felt comforted that God is with me no matter where I go, so I must never be afraid."

She smiled, and then said: "You will enjoy a better relationship with God if you make the Holy Spirit your Friend.

Keep doing what you did today, every day.

You will feel His presence around you more if you spend more time doing things that please God."

"You mean... doing things like singing or listening to praise and worship songs, meditating on Bible, and helping people?"

"Yes. Make it a habit to invite the Holy Spirit to be with you in everything you do, big or small, and He'll help you do things more easily. And He'll make you happy too," Mom said.

And I believed.

I was super-excited to know that I have an invisible Friend that I can talk to anytime. All I need to do is to invite Him.

Goodbye loneliness! Farewell boredom! Welcome happiness!

In a quiet place, I can tell the Holy Spirit anything and everything. I can tell Him how I feel. I can tell Him my needs, my wants, my dreams, and my secrets.

Whenever I don't believe in myself, the Holy Spirit will encourage me and remind me that I am a child of the most powerful God, the King of heaven and earth, who lives in me. I can do all things with His help!

I feel like I can fly and touch the skies. I have the power in me to do anything. And I have a Teacher who can teach me everything. With Him, nothing is impossible.

The Holy Spirit is my Enabler and Guide. He makes me want to do good and He leads me to live God's way-the right way. He bears fruit in me – fruit of love, peace, joy, patience, kindness, goodness, faithfulness, gentleness, and self-control, so that I can live a happy life.

Prayer: Dear Lord, please fill me with your Holy Spirit and let me walk in your power. Lead me in the right path every day of my life and let me your presence dwell with me all the days of my life. In the name of Jesus, I pray. Amen.

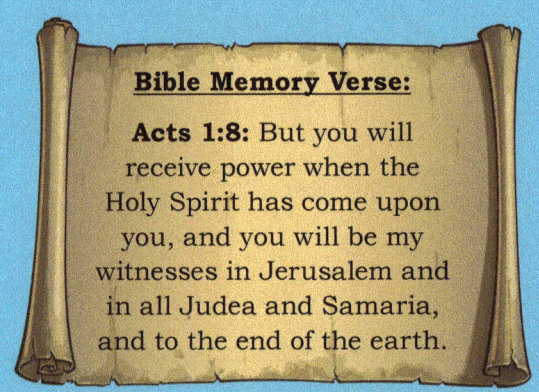

Bible Memory Verse:

Acts 1:8: But you will receive power when the Holy Spirit has come upon you, and you will be my witnesses in Jerusalem and in all Judea and Samaria, and to the end of the earth.

REFLECTION:

How can you relate personally with the Holy Spirit?

Think about something you find hard to do or think you can't do. Ask the Holy Spirit to teach and strengthen you.

5

THE FRUIT OF THE SPIRIT IS ... LOVE

Dear Friend,
I am excited to share with you what I've learnt about love, the first and most important fruit of the Spirit.

May the Holy Spirit help you understand as you read.

God is Love. He is our spiritual Father in heaven who provides everything we need. He gives us good gifts because He wants us to be happy.

All we need to do is ask God, in the name of Jesus, and we shall receive.

God loves human beings so much that He sent Jesus Christ, His only Son, from heaven to earth, to save us from serving an eternal punishment in hell after our lives here on earth.

You see, we are all born with a sinful nature. But we can't go to heaven with sin in us. But Jesus paid the full price for our sin in advance, by dying on the cross of Calvary. Jesus is the Savior of mankind.

No one has made a greater sacrifice. I'm amazed at God's love for us!

God is always ready to forgive all our sins, so that we can make it to heaven, but only when we are sorry and ask Him to forgive us each time.

Jesus saved me from my mean nature so that I can become a child God.

Mom told me that when I invited Jesus into my heart, to be my Lord, I was re-born into the family of God spiritually, and received the Holy Spirit. Jesus has become my new big brother, and He'll teach me the ways of God, with the help of the Holy Spirit that lives in me.

I must admit, I don't always mean to be naughty or mean – but sometimes, I just can't help it. I'm very thankful for this huge sacrifice that God made just to save someone like me.

At first, I didn't understand why.

Dad told me it is because I am special to God. You know, you are special to God too! That's why He made us in His image.

In return for the gift of His Son and eternal life in heaven, God just wants us to love Him back with all our hearts, and to love people the way He loves us, unconditionally.

Dad told me that loving God with all my heart means that I try to please God in everything I do - in the way I think, talk, act, and look.

God wants me to love people too - not because of who they are, or how they look, or what they have... but just because they too are created in God's image, just like me. They too are God's children; we are all brothers and sisters in God's big family on earth.

Sometimes, it can be hard to like people that look or act different because we don't know them or understand them. So, we tend to fear them and treat them unkindly.

But the Holy Spirit can change our spiritual hearts so that we see everyone like a child of God - no matter their color, or whether they are rich or poor.

He can help us show God's kind of love to people so that we treat everyone by the Golden rule - the way we want to be treated.

We must not judge people, or stay away from our schoolmates or neighbors just because they don't look or talk like us. Instead, God wants us to go closer, try to understand them and get to know them better. You'll find that people have a lot more in common than you know.

God will be pleased if we treat friends and strangers fairly, with love and respect.

If everyone on earth followed the Golden Rule, imagine what the world would be like... people won't hate or hurt each other, and the world would be a much safer and happier place to live in. The world would be awesome!

There are many ways that I can show love to God – by talking to Him regularly through prayers, obeying His instructions in the Bible, obeying my parents, praising, and worshipping Him with song and dance, and loving people.

God wants me to share His love with people – I can tell them that God loves them very much too. Some people don't know that God loves and cares for them whether they deserve it or not. Others don't believe it.

I can use my talents and skills to help people and tell them the good news that God loves them very much, and that Jesus can save them too.

God is pleased when we do these things. And I really want to please God.

Prayer: Dear God, thank you for loving me so much. Thank you for giving your only Son, Jesus, to die for me. Please forgive my sins and save me. I want to follow you. Teach me how to love you more with all my heart and how to love people. In the name of Jesus, I pray. Amen.

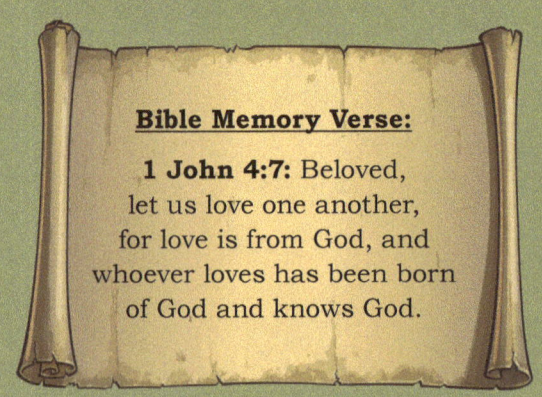

Bible Memory Verse:

1 John 4:7: Beloved, let us love one another, for love is from God, and whoever loves has been born of God and knows God.

REFLECTION:

Do you believe that God loves you? Do you love God?

In what ways can you show love to God?

List three other ways can you show love to people this week.

6

THE FRUIT OF THE SPIRIT IS ... JOY, PEACE

Friend, I learnt something else: that the Holy Spirit gives joy and peace.

Whenever I am feeling sad, frustrated, or discouraged, the Holy Spirit comforts me - He makes me feel better.

One time I felt very frustrated because I did not remember to follow mom's instruction to tidy up my room. Playing was so much more fun – so I kept on playing. And the time just flew by...

Mom was mad at me, and I was mad at myself. I convinced myself that I was no good and that I could never become responsible - it was just hard to do the right thing.

So, I told mom just that. "I can't," I said through my tears.

"I can never become responsible. It's just too hard!"

A fresh stream of tears flowed from my eyes as I sat at the edge of my bed with my hands across my chest, rocking myself back and forth.

"Nonsense!" Mom replied. "Don't you say that again, child. Of course, you can. You will grow up and become a responsible man. Now, repeat after me: I am a child of God. And I can do all things through Christ who strengthens me."

I didn't repeat – I was too frustrated to obey.

Then, in between my tears, I looked up at my mom's face and saw it change from being mad to calm. She closed her eyes.

"Dear God," she whispered, "please give me the patience and wisdom to help Your child."

Then she was quiet, eyes still closed, maybe for a few more minutes.

Maybe she was praying in her mind.

Finally, when she opened her eyes, she spoke calmly to me.

She said: "Listen, Alex - nobody is good at everything. Everybody has a weakness – something that they struggle to do well.

However, one important key to success is finding a way to overcome your weakness. And God can help you if you ask Him." She paused for a moment.

"And you know... your thoughts - about being no good - are not from God, Alex," she added.

"You see, Child, God only inspires good thoughts. It is hard to hear God's voice when you're very angry, frustrated or discouraged.

Such bad thoughts are big lies that the devil plants in your heart, to steal your joy and keep you stuck, so you don't achieve great things.

But the devil is the father of lies! You must never believe him.

Here's what God says about you, Alex, which you must believe: you are made in God's image. You are beautiful. You have the power to do great things that you don't even know you can do yet. But in time, you will, my love. This is the truth from God's word.

When things are tough, when you feel angry or frustrated, remember that your Helper is with you - so you ought to try and try again. Never give up!"

I totally believed her.

Mom reminded me that the Holy Spirit is my Helper - that He could take away the frustration I was feeling.

At this point, I was paying full attention because I didn't like the way I felt – it was a mix of anger, pain, sadness, and helplessness - all together; like sea waves bombarding the walls of my heart. I wished the awful feeling would go away.

"Say after me," Mom said again. "Holy Spirit help me".

This time, I felt like repeating it, so I did: "Holy Spirit, help me," I whispered.

Suddenly, it seemed like sunlight rays had invaded my troubled heart and displaced the darkness that had occupied it for a moment. I felt happy deep in my heart - the sadness had totally disappeared.

I stopped crying. I was quiet. I felt calm - I felt peace. No more wild waves bombarding the walls of my heart - just peace.

We kept silent for a few more minutes.

"How do you feel now?" Mom asked. I paused to think.

"I actually feel happy now," I replied, through a smile, not understanding what had just happened.

"Thank you, Lord," Mom responded. "Now you know what to do whenever you are feeling angry, frustrated or discouraged."

She explained that God had answered my prayer. He had replaced my sadness with joy and had brought peace to my troubled heart.

That made sense to me. I could feel the difference. I wondered how that had happened.

God had used Mom to remind me of God's truths about me. And I ditched the devil's lies and believed in God's truths. So, when I had prayed, the Holy Spirit did a spiritual transformation in my heart. Peace trooped in, and joy followed right after. I felt like a new person.

I really liked this new feeling. I wanted it to stay.

Laying on my bed that night, before I fell asleep, I muttered the words:

"Dear Lord, thank you for using Mom to make me feel better today. Please remind me of what to do the next time the devil tries to steal my joy and peace again. In Jesus' name I pray. Amen."

Prayer: Dear Holy Spirit, help me grow in the fruit of joy and peace. Please help me to always remember God's truth about who I am. And teach me how to invite your peace and joy whenever my heart is troubled or sad. I ask these things in the name of Jesus. Amen.

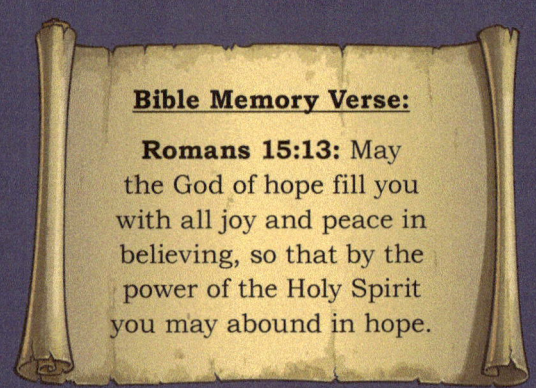

Bible Memory Verse:

Romans 15:13: May the God of hope fill you with all joy and peace in believing, so that by the power of the Holy Spirit you may abound in hope.

7

THE FRUIT OF THE SPIRIT IS ... PATIENCE

I think of patience as the ability to handle difficult issues and people without getting upset.

"Patience is a virtue," Mom always says. "The patient dog eats the fattest bone."

I know that for many children like me, patience can be a hard behavior to develop. I don't like to wait – I usually want things right now.

Does this happen to you sometimes?

For example, when I'm hungry and dinner is not yet ready, I tend to be impatient. I would ask Mom anxiously: "is the food ready yet?" every minute or so, she says, until I get it.

But I'm learning to be patient as I grow older. Nowadays while waiting, I do something to take my mind away from what is causing me to be anxious.

For example, while waiting for the food to be ready, I could do a chore, read a book, take a shower, or play. This strategy has worked for me.

Another area where I am learning to practice more patience is with people. Before, when my baby brother messed up my room after I had tidied up, or when a friend intruded into my personal space when I wanted to be alone, I would get upset and yell at them.

Now, I understand that they don't always mean to upset me. So, I try to stay calm. Sometimes, I tell my friend, calmly, that I want to be alone.

With my brother, I try to ignore him when he's naughty, or just walk away.

I have learned to show patience. Patience is a way to show love to people.

God is always patient with me even when I am being a difficult child. He made everyone different so I must be patient when dealing with other people.

Another area where I tend to be impatient is when I feel like God is not answering my prayer quickly enough.

"God's timing is different from ours," Mom said. "Plus, sometimes His answer could be 'Wait' – if the time is not right, or 'No' – if He sees that what you are asking for could hurt you."

"Really?" I replied, surprised. "I thought God will give us anything, if we ask in the name of Jesus?"

"Well, think about it this way, my love," she responded patiently, "would I give you my car keys to drive just because you asked for it nicely?"

"Maybe?" I teased, even though I knew where she was going with this.

"Well, I won't. Because you are too young to drive. You could crash the car and hurt yourself.

Similarly when you pray, like a good father, God will only give you good gifts.

So, whatever His response will be, you must wait patiently and trust that God will always act in your best interest. He will give you the right thing at the right time and it will bring you joy."

I heard Mom, but I don't think I liked what I heard. I want God to say 'Yes' to all my prayer requests.

But Mom is older and wiser. I guess, I'll understand better when I grow up.

Prayer: Dear Lord, thank you for always showing patience to me even when I'm being difficult. Please teach me how to handle every situation with patience. And teach me how to treat everyone with patience. In the name of Jesus, I pray. Amen.

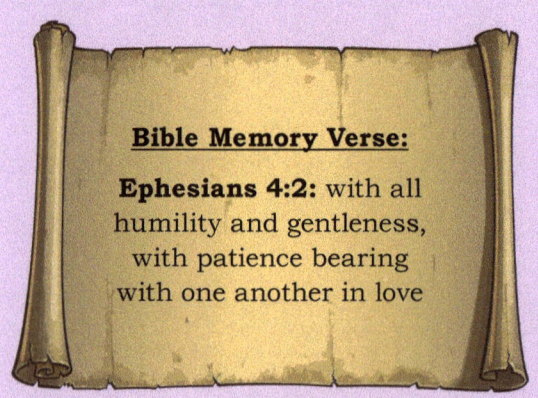

Bible Memory Verse:

Ephesians 4:2: with all humility and gentleness, with patience bearing with one another in love

REFLECTION:

Think about a situation or a person that you did not handle with patience. What can you do differently next time to show patience?

8

THE FRUIT OF THE SPIRIT IS ... KINDNESS, GOODNESS

Simply put, kindness is when you feel like being nice or doing something good for someone.
Kindness is also when you feel empathy or compassion for someone – and you want to do something nice for someone.

Goodness, on the other hand, is the action that follows the feeling of kindness. When you do a good deed for someone, especially when they don't deserve it, then you have shown goodness.

Acting in a kind manner is goodness. Showing kindness is doing good.

One day, Mom and I were driving to the local grocery store when we stopped at a traffic light. While waiting for the traffic lights to turn green, we saw a man in dirty clothes and old, torn shoes. He held a piece of cardboard paper with words that read:" Homeless. Hungry. Anything will help."

I felt sorry for him – that he didn't have a house to live in like I did and that he couldn't afford to eat.

Mom must have felt compassion for him too. She reached into her purse, quickly pulled some money out of her wallet, then pulled down the driver's window and stretched out the money towards him.

Seeing her move, the stranger immediately ran towards us, grabbed the money and with a big smile on his face, he said, "Thank you. God bless you."

The lights turned green and Mom drove off.

Mom is kind – she was moved to do a good deed to a total stranger.

I felt happy for the stranger too. Now, he could buy himself some food.

Another time, my little brother was feeling very frustrated. As a result, he ran to his room and started crying frantically. For a long time, he kept crying, and won't stop.

I felt bad for him.

After a while, I approached him and told him that he was the best brother in the whole world. I also told him that I love him.

Almost immediately, he stopped crying and smiled at me.

I smiled back and gave him a big hug.

He laughed. He was happy now. I felt good that I had helped him feel better.

There have also been times when I did something mean to someone or disobeyed Mom or Dad. Then I felt sorry right after and apologized.

Dad said that the Holy Spirit makes us feel bad when we hurt God or people. He convicts us when we do wrong and nudges us to ask for forgiveness so that we can make it right with God and the people that we hurt.

When you do the right thing and make peace with people, God takes away your guilty feeling and gives you peace and joy.

God wants us to be kind to each other. He wants us to care about other people's pain – family and strangers alike - and be moved to help them.

I learned that acts of goodness go full circle and return to you. God can use me to bless somebody. And He can use somebody else to bless me. My good deed could be an answer to somebody's prayer and vice versa.

I am encouraged to keep doing good to everyone I come across. So, help me Lord God.

Prayer: Dear Lord, thank you for blessing me. Let the fruit of kindness grow in me. Please empower me for the rest of my life to never get tired of doing good things. In Jesus' name I pray. Amen.

Bible Memory Verse:

Galatians 6:9: And let us not grow weary of doing good, for in due season we will reap, if we do not give up.

REFLECTION:

In what other ways can you show kindness to people?

Ask God for an opportunity to show kindness to someone this week. Write down your good deeds every week. Tell God about them.

9
THE FRUIT OF THE SPIRIT IS ... FAITHFULNESS

Do you know the word faithfulness? Dad explained faithfulness to me. It means sticking with someone or something, or doing something repeatedly and unfailingly, no matter the situation.

To be faithful to God means that God can trust you to keep believing in Him, and not worship another god, both in good times and in bad times without failing.

You see, God is jealous when we make someone or something else our priority over Him. Like when we choose to spend more time doing other things but spend only a little time with Him. He loves us and wants us to spend more time in His presence, to build a stronger bond with Him.

Marriage is one example of faithfulness that I can think of. Mom and Dad have been married for many years now and have stayed faithful to each other. They trust each other and have grown to know and love each other more. I'm sure that they have had fights before and encountered tough times.

But through it all, they chose to remain committed to their promise of love and to stick with each other through thick and thin.

Just like spouses in marriage, God wants us to be faithful to Him. Staying faithful to God is proof that we love Him back.

At first, I thought faithfulness sounded like a hard to do, that it was meant for adults only. Afterall, it requires love and lots of patience.

But Dad said obedience and consistency are important keys to faithfulness.

"Even children can practice faithfulness," Dad said. "Think about school, Alex. Ever since Kindergarten, you've been attending school every school day. In good weather, under the rain and in the snow – you didn't miss school except on days when you fell sick. And even then, you would return to school as soon as you felt better.

I remember how on many mornings, when you were tired, you would still try to wake up early and go to school. You have attended school faithfully and as a result, your teachers now count on you to be in class every day because you have proven to be reliable.

You see, faithfulness requires big sacrifices and endurance. Remember when you would return from school every day, and had to do your homework, even when you were tired or didn't feel like it?"

"Oh yes, I do. But I'm thankful for you and Mom. You help me with my homework and always encourage me when I want to give up."

"We are thankful for you too, Child," replied Dad.

'I'll tell you more. Every now and then, God will test your faith in Him. Do you know why Abraham is called the Father of Faith in the Bible?" Dad asked.

"Why?" I asked curiously.

"Because he passed one of God's toughest tests of faith. God asked him to sacrifice His beloved son, Isaac, to Him and Abraham obeyed, until God Himself stopped him.

God was so impressed that Abraham chose to obey Him, when given such a tough choice, that He gave Abraham blessings that have persisted through generations after him. As a result of his faithfulness, today we can sing: 'Abraham's blessings are mine,' Dad said.

This made sense. I attend school faithfully. I love learning and playing with friends in school. School has become a thing I do constantly - a habit.

Similarly, I can show faithfulness to God by consistently worshipping Him alone, even when people tease me about it. I can pray to God every day, go to church, and try always to obey God's instructions, as well as my parents' instructions.

I must stay away from things that can cause God to be upset with me. And I must never choose to disobey God and rather listen to bad advice from friends or anyone else.

God will be disappointed if I do. And I never want to disappoint God.

But if, along the line, I fail to obey God or I get tired, Dad says God is patient and forgiving of our mistakes. In moments like these, I must quickly repent and ask God to forgive me and strengthen me to do better the next time.

God will always forgive me if I am sincerely sorry for doing wrong and do my best not to sin again. God is a good and merciful Father.

The Holy Spirit is my Helper. He can enable me to overcome temptation and empower me to do the right thing always.

Prayer: Dear Lord, forgive me for the times when I have not been faithful to you.

Please give me a constant and willing spirit. Give me the power to always resist the temptation to disobey your instructions or to follow bad advice. In the name of Jesus, I pray. Amen.

Bible Memory Verse:

Genesis 26:4-5: I will multiply your descendants as the stars of heaven, and will give your descendants all these lands; and by your descendants all the nations of the earth shall be blessed; because Abraham obeyed Me and kept My charge, My commandments, My statutes and My laws.

REFLECTION:

In what ways can you personally show faithfulness to God? Start with one thing and commit to doing it constantly this month. Then pick up the next thing and do the same next month.

10

THE FRUIT OF THE SPIRIT IS ... GENTLENESS

I used to think that gentleness meant that someone was calm or spoke softly.

But I learnt that gentleness goes way beyond just how we speak. It also has to do with how we think or act in response to someone or something.

Sometimes, children throw tantrums when they are angry or feeling frustrated. They would say mean words or think about doing a mean thing, even if they didn't eventually do it.

Some would respond with an insult after their schoolmate insulted them, or they would plan a revenge in their mind for a later time.

To be honest, I may be guilty of snatching or hiding my brother's toy at least once after he got me upset.

"Such violent reactions are not how God wants His children to behave," Mom would respond.

"But how come they occur so naturally in us?" I cried out in confusion.

Mom said that our bad instincts are a result of our naturally mean nature. Most often, we need to learn the right way to respond that will please God.

God can change your violent nature into a gentle one if you ask Him for help.

She taught me a strategy to help me respond with gentleness whenever I was tempted to react violently: **STOP** ...**THINK (PRAY)** ...and then **ACT**.

I tried it recently. I was angry when Mom asked me to stop playing and to go do my house chore instead. I wanted to walk away and slam my room door in response, to express my frustration.

As I looked up at her, I stopped for a moment, and considered the consequences of such an action - Mom would feel disrespected, and I could get grounded from screen time for a while. Clearly, no good result could come from me fighting back.

I needed to calm down – but my heart was pumping fast in anger. First, I counted, 1, 2, ... 9, 10. But that didn't work – I think I counted too fast.

I took a deep breath in frustration. Then I remembered what Mom would do whenever she was getting impatient with us.

"Lord, help me," I said under my breath.

Suddenly, I had an idea – it would be so much easier if I just obeyed Mom's instruction. After my chores, I could come right back and play.

This plan was more reasonable. Mom would be happy, and I won't get grounded – everybody will win. Why didn't I think about this earlier?

I think the Holy Spirit just inspired me with this bright idea.

"Ok, Mom," I responded calmly. "I'll go do my chores first." I walked past her into the kitchen and swept the floor.

Mom was very surprised. She was expecting me to put up a fight and argue with her as usual - anything but a gentle and obedient response.

But on this day, I chose gentleness – I did the right thing. When I prayed, the Holy Spirit inspired me and led me to choose God's way.

As a result, I avoided getting into a fight with Mom or getting grounded. Win – win!

Gentleness helps us live in peace with people and results in joy.

Prayer: Dear Lord, please give me a gentle spirit. Teach me how to calm down whenever I am provoked and lead me to choose the right way to act every time. In the name of Jesus, I pray. Amen.

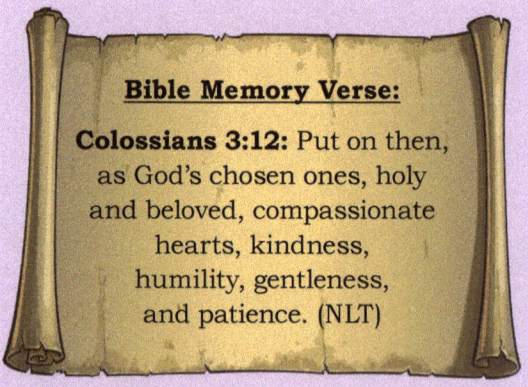

Bible Memory Verse:

Colossians 3:12: Put on then, as God's chosen ones, holy and beloved, compassionate hearts, kindness, humility, gentleness, and patience. (NLT)

REFLECTION:

Why is gentleness important?

Give an example of a situation where you can apply the "Stop, Think (Pray), then Act" strategy.

11

THE FRUIT OF THE SPIRIT IS ... SELF-CONTROL

Friend, are you still there?
We're down to the last, but not the least virtue of the Fruit of the Spirit, which is self-control.

I think self-control is the ability to control your mind and body. It is self-discipline—intentionally applying yourself to do the right thing every time.

Anyone or anything that you cannot control will control you.

God has given us the freedom to do anything, but not everything is good for us.

Applying self-control can keep us from falling into temptation, or the trap of the devil.

There are some areas in my life where I'm learning to practice more self-control. Maybe you can relate to some of my struggles too.

Sometimes, I find it incredibly hard to stop thinking about food. In times like these, I could direct my mind to think about something else instead, like... a happy song, a joke or story.

Another time, I got so excited by the sight of food that I ate more than my tummy could take. Then I ended up with a tummy ache.

Oh! And how about the times when I would snap and yell at my toddler brother because I was upset. The anger was clearly in control of my actions.

But if I can stop and think about how bad my tummy would hurt if I ate too much, then that could cause me to control my excessive appetite. Or, if I considered that my brother would be hurt when I yelled at him, then I could respond differently.

When these tips don't work, I always fall back on my Helper. The Holy Spirit can help me control my emotions, my thoughts, my desires - anything.

The strategy of STOP, THINK (PRAY), then ACT also works when I'm trying to practice self-control.

Like one time when I got discouraged and felt like giving up on my piano lesson. My impatience grew as weeks turned into months, and months turned into years. Finally, I couldn't keep my emotion a secret anymore.

"Why do I have to do piano all the time?" I whined at Mom. "I hate attending piano class every week. I hate practicing every day. Plus, I still have to do homework. I don't even want to be a musician when I grow up!"

This time around, Mom took me to my piano teacher to respond to me. Miss Kayla took me to a quiet room and explained the many benefits of learning music.

"It's like learning a new language," she said, "music helps your brain make complex connections quicker. It can improve your self-confidence and even your school performance in other subjects."

"Alex," Miss Kayla continued, "you are really good at playing the piano. And I know you can do anything you set your mind to. Don't give up on this and in time, you will be glad you stayed the course."

That sounded like a good reason to keep learning the piano. I want to be smarter and perform better at school.

Plus, Miss Kayla thinks I'm good at playing the piano. I think she's right. I can do this!

The next time Mr. Discouragement knocked on the door of my heart, urging me to hate piano class, I heard a small voice reminding me that learning piano will make me smarter. And that I have the power to do anything I set my mind to do.

I realized that usually, when I stopped and thought about the benefits, I was able to control my emotions. The anger calmed down and the discouragement turned into a renewed desire to attend piano class.

And at the end, I was happy that I attended the piano lesson that day.

When we show self-control, we show evidence that the Holy Spirit lives in us and that He has transformed us one step closer into God's nature.

Prayer: Dear Lord, thank you for your Holy Spirit that helps me control myself so that I can be the good child you want me to be. Please take away anything that will keep your Holy Spirit away from me and let the Fruit of the Holy Spirit keep growing in me. In Jesus' mighty name I pray. Amen.

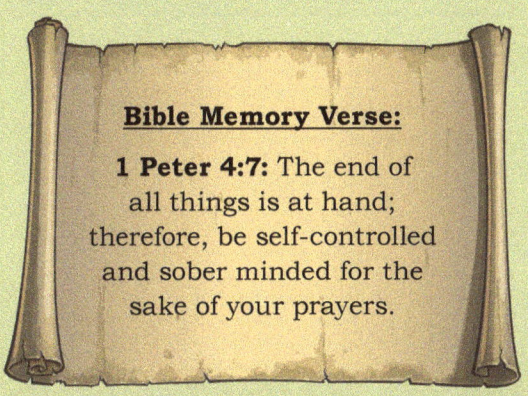

Bible Memory Verse:

1 Peter 4:7: The end of all things is at hand; therefore, be self-controlled and sober minded for the sake of your prayers.

REFLECTION:

Think of an area in your life where you need the Holy Spirit to help you apply self-control. Ask Him to help you now.

How can the Holy Spirit help you apply self-control?

12

AFTERWORD

Dear Friend,
I sincerely hope that you have had fun on this exciting adventure, learning more about the Holy Spirit and the Fruit of the Spirit.

I'm so glad that I made a new friend with the person of the Holy Spirit and I'm also excited about how He is already changing me to become the beautiful person that God created me to be and to do good deeds.

Without the Holy Spirit, it is difficult to continue doing good. I can't wait to grow more in the Fruit of the Spirit.

Can you describe the Fruit of the Spirit mentioned in Galatians 5:22-23?

The Bible describes nine virtues that make up the Fruit of the Spirit: love, joy, peace, patience, kindness, goodness, faithfulness, gentleness, and self-control. These virtues indicate the presence of the Holy Spirit in the child of God.

The stronger and more consistent my relationship is with the Holy Spirit, the more virtues will He produce in me.

The greatest of these virtues is love.

If I love God with all my heart, I must always obey Him, and do His will.

God's will is the best choice for me and will always lead to a happy life.

Also, if I love my neighbors as I love myself, then I must treat them with love and kindness, just the way I want to be treated. This is how God wants us all to act.

I believe that if we all act lovingly towards one another, friends and strangers alike, then the world can become a better place. No more hate, no more fear, no more fighting and killing each other, no wars, none of these.

Because, in time, love will always conquer hate.

Friend, may the love of God prevail in your heart and mine, and overflow to spread the goodness of God all over the world.

The Holy Spirit is my Friend and Helper. He connects me with Jesus and helps me think and act like Jesus would, so that I can become the beautiful and wonderful person that God created me to be.

He changes me into a better person, so that I can live a peaceful and happy life here on earth, just the way God wants. He will continue to lead and guide me to do the right thing every time if I keep trusting and obeying Him.

The Holy Spirit can help you too, become the beautiful person that God created you to be. He can help you bear good fruit… if you believe.

Do you believe?

Then pray like this:

My Father in heaven, thank you for loving me so much.

Lord, Jesus, I believe in you. Please come and rule my heart.

Holy Spirit, please lead me and guide me in the way of God.

In the mighty name of Jesus, I pray.

Say Amen.

THE END

Child of God, smile – Jesus loves you!
Arise, now, and explore the realm of possibilities ahead of you. The world is waiting for you to manifest in your full potential – to display the glory of God. Therefore, let your light shine bright for the world to see.

With Love,
~Judith Tamasang Jogwuia

Judith Tamasang Jogwuia currently serves at Recreation Fire and Miracles Ministries as an assisting pastor, where she has been privileged to teach Sunday School and Bible Studies, almost weekly, since 2015.

She has a passion for teaching the Word of God and strongly believes that when we invest in teaching God's Word to our children early, they will grow with self-confidence and purpose to become good moral citizens. They will also be well equipped to handle the challenges that life will inevitably bring their way, with the help of God the Holy Spirit.

She and her family currently reside in the Twin Cities area in Minnesota, USA.

www.ingramcontent.com/pod-product-compliance
Lightning Source LLC
LaVergne TN
LVHW051226070526
838200LV00057B/4619